A collection of poetry meant to uplift and inspire. In the name of the Glory of God and His love.

PAUL D. SIMS

Breathe In Calvary Publishing LLC.

Copyright © 2023 by Breathe In Calvary Publishing LLC.

All rights reserved. This collection of poetry or any portion thereof may not be reproduced or used in any manner whatsoever without the written consent of the publisher or Author, except in the use of brief quotations for a book review.

All information provided in the pages of this book are that developed to provide growth for those who read it. The information provided is from the direct experience of the Author and thus may be taken as so.

-Breathe In Calvary Publishing LLC-

When God Speaks

CONTENTS

Verse

Title Page

Dedication

About the Author

Section One (14)

Section Two (21)

Section Three (21)

Section Four (17)

Section Five (4)

End

Paul D. Sims

PSALM 45:1

When God Speaks

Paul D. Sims

Paul D. Sims

DEDICATION

All glory be to GOD. The one who led me to write these poems in His name.

ABOUT THE AUTHOR

    Paul D. Sims is a classic individual with a love for spreading the peace and Glory of God. In 2008, he felt influenced by the Holy Spirit to run for office. Even despite a legitimate fear of speaking in public. As he spoke, it resonated with many people. He continued to do God's will.

    Paul lives his life serving our Father, and thus felt led to sing. As he sang, he also felt the need to write songs. This then evolved into composition notebooks filled with poetry as God directly spoke to his heart.

Paul D. resides in Missouri where he has a beautiful family, farm, and continued drive to bring God's children back to His side. He worships with light in his heart and supports those around him with his dedication to the Lord.

Paul D. Sims

SECTION ONE

1

Grow where God has planted you.

With the faith of healing, glory, and light be given to His name.

2

We have nothing but pen and paper,

But that is all we care to use for Him.

Write, and see what he will do,

With just as much as pen and paper,

He will spread the truth.

3

Sweet child of mine,

Come sit and listen,

To what I am to say.

For some, I may use you,

In my own special way.

For I save you,

For a special day.

To fulfill my way,

And bring glory to my name.

I told you many years ago,

That you were mine,

And here my promise stands.

I will stay with you till the end of time.

4

Time it seems is standing still for me.

When you are carrying my spirit,

For it seems like there is no time at all.

For it is all yours.

What you give to me,

I give back to use for your glory.

That is all for if not,

Then for you,

Oh, that is just as you want for thee.

When God Speaks

5

Do you know my name?

I need only to see if you know my name.

I made this home for you.

Do you know my name?

I made the climb to talk.

Do you know my name?

I was down, I wear a crown of thorns.

Do you know my name?

I took nails for you.

Was it in vain?

Do you know my name?

On this third day I rose again,

why do you sigh against this name?

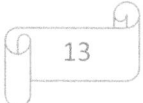

You sing songs in this land,

For I am its light.

Often you look for tomorrow.

I am its way out.

Do you know my name?

Of your song, I am a true guide to you for tomorrow.

Do you know my name?

My love will shine on your tomorrow.

My love will shine on you.

Remember my name,

As my love flows through your veins,

Can you remember my name?

As my breath runs through you,

Can you remember my name?

As my peace runs through your veins,

Can you remember my name?

When God Speaks

As my Spirit guides your love,

Jesus is my name.

Why don't you call on my name?

I'll show you what it means to fly.

Know my name, and fly with me, into the clouds.

Meeting me, on the clouds.

My name is Jesus, the savior of the world.

The savior of you.

Remember the name,

and you will be destined with me,

for always and forever.

6

Why can't they hear that it's getting close to the end?

It's time to find their way in,

For like in the days of Noah,

It will all soon come to the end.

Not rain this time,

But fire that will burn it all away.

Why can't they hear the call?

For soon they will fall,

To a place no one wants.

A place they were not made for.

If they do not listen,

Then soon they go alone.

It is easy if they take it day by day,

When God Speaks

Or even moreover,

Minute by minute,

But listen closely,

to hear our father's call,

arising in triumph before they all fall.

7

They say tomorrow is not promised,

But yet it is- or is it not?

If I truly believe in him who returns,

It's him who controls the clock.

Absent here,

Is present there,

So tomorrow is always coming.

Just as we are always in the now,

Not in the then and when.

But in has always been for Him,

The future, past, and present.

He ran the clock which never ends,

In His will,

So that we may never worry of it.

8

Look at me now,

From what I was- to what I am.

Because of you,

I am what I am.

So much better than I should be,

For your grace has taken place.

Grace has replaced what I would have been,

With what you wanted me to be.

You never left me,

Even when I was not lovable.

Change you have made with your grace,

Despite every one of my sins.

Paul D. Sims

Can't stay in place for it grows at a rapid pace,

Now I have been given a chance.

I could win the race,

To stay forever in your place.

Perfect I am not,

Nor ever will I ever be.

Lonely as I am,

But yet you always hear my plea

.

9

Why do they blame he who is without blame?

When truly it is of them,

For they do these things.

Things that cause pain forever throughout eternity.

Let us instead do what can bring us peace,

To be ours for eternity.

Hardships will come and go.

So, learn what is to be.

Help others to see its peace,

That is to be for our eternity.

Love is not hard to show,

But can bring those into reigning eternity.

Paul D. Sims

Grace is given freely,

For you and me.

His love is given to us,

As we should give love to others.

Let us all reach and find the way to him for all eternity.

It soon will be ours really,

We should not differently be.

The other is no place for any to be,

So remember it is you,

You who cause him,

To split your blissful eternity.

Instead, to be cast out,

Where rain, sorrow, pain, and discomfort- all will be.

10

You let me see with your eyes.

What a sight!

Beauty abounds everywhere you turn,

Yet it's ugliness made within.

How can you stand how heavy it is?

Help me to get mixed up in you.

Let me hear some of what you hear.

Oh, how good and bad is mixed in.

I cannot stand what is within.

You helped me to feel how truly sweet it would be,

When I will always be with thee.

Overwhelmed by you,

You hold me.

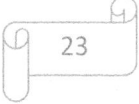

Paul D. Sims

> I want to return to what is,
> I want to return with thee.

11

So strong,

Yet so tender,

Your hands be so sweet.

It's a feeling words cannot express.

What I feel,

The spirit comes up,

As yet ever so strongly,

And wind in your hand flows,

So soft and light,

While also stern and tough.

So, trust in you,

How easy that be,

And at times may be so hard,

Yet I always find peace with you.

Now maybe they will see why I am ready to leave,

Long as I be with thee.

So, in your eyes,

I will always be.

Please let them see what we'll be,

So surely they will come to thee.

12

Free To Fly

When you are with me,

I am free,

So free.

I feel like I am flying.

Flying because I am free,

With you in my dream.

We are flying with you,

Held in your hand,

We fly thanks to you.

Oh, how you set my spirit free.

Free to fly away with you.

When with you I need nothing,

Because you give me so much.

I am flying with you,

So, nothing,

No nothing is like being with you.

Oh, how I long for those times,

The times I am full of you.

Yes, I have in the past,

Done things not of you.

Things they say,

Make you sigh.

Oh, how wrong they were,

Nothing can make me fly like with you.

So, please stay with me for now.

Yes I know soon it will be time,

Time to die or fly,

Only to you.

When God Speaks

Flying to you has no loss of time,
Dying is but a blink of the eye.
Only to blink again and forever fly,
Within your light.

13

Hello my friend,

There you are again.

What's that?

You have always been here?

Oh, it's me that forgot you.

Yet you never go away,

Now I see,

But not with my eyes,

For the eyes can deceive.

You see.

For what is, may not be as it seems.

Things may be forever,

Yet look as if heart and soul pieces have fallen away,

When God Speaks

As if lost forever,

But when you are what is, has been, and will be,

You love all now I see.

The heart and soul pieces come back together,

A constant and unyielding tether.

14

I don't hold the sun,

The moon,

Or all its stars,

But I know who does.

I have no silver,

Nor a platter,

But why should it matter?

For I know who holds all that exists,

And who made all this world,

So, if your problem is vast,

And you have no plan or method,

Turn to the one,

Who can write your life in a new direction.

SECTION TWO

1

If you feel alone,

Go into the moonlight.

Let it kiss you on your face.

Now you've been kissed by the father,

He is the light of night and day.

His love like no other,

His love for all of us,

His love bigger than all other,

His love for always and forever.

The love of this father given for all,

So strong and yet so tender.

So firm and yet so gentle.

Given so complete and sweet,

When God Speaks

How sweet the kiss that's given by thee,

The light bliss and so soft yet let us see,

Where we be.

Moon bright,

Kissing each differently.

Like the love of the father,

Different for each,

Who believe,

Yet given freely.

The love given by He,

It's truest of all.

Purest that can ever be.

So, prepare soon,

We will forever be,

With he who we felt,

That love first delt.

Paul D. Sims

Oh, to be with the father,

His love surrounding us,

For all time soon.

Soon to be loved with he,

The father,

And kissed by thee,

Just as we were by the moon beams.

2

If there is one thing missing in my life,

It's the moonlight shining on me bright.

For if there is that,

I feel the kiss.

A kiss of the moonlight on my face.

A kiss of the loving father upon me,

Telling me of a love so great.

So great above all,

A love far from small,

In itself will bring life to be.

A love that's so hard,

So difficult to describe,

So full,

So deep.

Paul D. Sims

A love that beams,

.

Like no other love.
A love that will bring,
Grace to its lover,
A love for the sister,
A love for the brother.
A love for what is,
What is to be,
and what has been.
What a love,
So just yet so gentle,
So strong yet so simple,
A love that is felt so deeply,
To those who have chosen to receive.

3

When I saw its light,

I gave my life,

For something.

Something more than I could comprehend.

Something bigger than I could understand.

I could see with my eyes,

But I couldn't see with my heart.

Yesterday and forever,

The plan will go on.

No matter what,

We are meant to accept.

We are participants,

Leading and living life obediently.

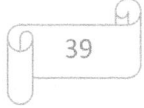

As plain as life can seem to be,

It goes on,

No matter how we act,

For all mankind love.

True love is it's key,

To the plan, His plan.

The love of our father,

To the Son who was sacrificed,

And the spirit who cries out,

For God the father forever,

This love will be in existence,

Longer than time itself,

Forever love of the father is.

The love that is like no other,

The love that gives a glow on all things.

Love that gets you through all your tomorrow's,

When God Speaks

Love strong enough to turn this world's sorrows.

Yet it's love that flows so full,

All will soon know.

The love and to feel the Father.

4

I look and see,

The fire came down.

I see my sister in Christ,

Shaking like a leaf,

On her face a glow,

Like few will ever see.

As the fire of He,

That will always be, engulfing her.

The love of He,

Is upon her stronger,

Than you would think,

It could ever be.

The love of the father for His children.

The love without bounds,

When God Speaks

And forever to be.

Her lips part,

Mouth gaping open,

A voice drifting out so broken,

Yet so sweet,

So strong and complete.

A language so beautiful,

The ear wants to hear.

A song straight from Heaven.

Soon one translator,

Giving wisdom,

And knowledge to all who will listen.

These words you see are from He.

Who will always and forever be.

The one who has always been.

The creator who was and will always be.

So strong the spirit,

Paul D. Sims

Fall He upon her,

All around she could feel,

But me, I could not speak,

A spread smile in the wake of my voice,

For I called her my little sister you see.

The father using her voice was such a joy to me.

5

Why leave it in your mind?

When it is so kind.

Tell what is on your mind,

Is it about the one so kind?

Tell about Jesus,

The one who loves all,

Tell about Jesus,

Tell it right now.

Tell it right here.

Time goes so quickly,

We have so little left.

Paul D. Sims

Tell of His kindness,

Right here, right now.

Tell of His vow.

It will mean so much to them,

Tell them how.

It's for everyone now.

Don't leave this message for tomorrow.

It's for right here and right now.

Go tell of His kindness,

His love and His vow.

It means everything now.

Yes, it means everything now.

6

I thought I knew so well,

Oh, how I let you go away.

You were supposed to be inside,

A part of me never to fade away.

A part of me I thought,

Was a whole plan caught.

That's how I understood,

But I never really did.

I never understood you well.

Inside me,

You were always,

Paul D. Sims

For the years to be.

You hadn't changed the plan.

Why did I misunderstand?

Looking for you I did,

When all I had to do,

Was talk to you.

Then the part of you that was,

Lie still inside of me,

Never to go away.

For we can never leave you,

And you never left my side.

You bring us back to life,

With a breath so sweet.

When God Speaks

Beyond the twisted lies,

I want you to get inside and hide you.

Thank you for the patience,

You have in me,

Even when I turn the other cheek.

I never want to feel again,

The absence of thee.

Thank you for this love,

Such a forgiving dove.

Why did I not understand?

When told that thee could be in one,

It meant that you could be in everyone,

And still be in me.

Paul D. Sims

Thank you for this joy,

You have given me,

Oh, this gift of thee.

No better way to be,

Than with you for eternity.

Please guard me from my pride,

So, I may never be,

To get between,

You and me again,

Now I understand,

In all,

So much better to be,

With thee till the end.

7

If you could only see what I see,

With my eyes.

Think with only one explanation,

It happens like,

This just can't be.

Imagination, it happens just as prayers are sent.

The request for just that thing,

If you would believe.

You would see with your eyes,

Even if it could not be explained,

In any other way that, it's a miracle.

Just a miracle from heaven above.

Oh when our belief abounds,

Stronger than anything before.

We would see things of God.

A love from the Father given,

To children so freely for those who believe,

In what He can do that no other can.

8

It only hurts to breathe,

When your not next to me.

For without you,

I am not me.

Without you,

I cannot see.

Not even what is,

In front of me.

Oh, the love,

I have for thee.

If simply felt,

Cannot be certain in me.

A love so deep,

That without you it is hard to be.

My love for thee is so deep,

I can barely see without thee.

I ask, why can all not see?

All the love for thee our God.

You sent your son to save us,

Just men and women,

Nothing like Jesus.

For he is the greatest savior,

That can be,

A savior sent for me,

When God Speaks

No savior is greater than your son, is He.

You sent Him, your son,

To save we.

Love, a love greater,

Cannot be.

A love that saves me.

A love that fixes we,

What love He has for she and he.

What love we should give He,

To the one that will always be,

The one with love so deep,

You see,

That He gave,

Paul D. Sims

What was,

Of He, a son if the greatest,

That will ever be.

The God of all that is,

And will ever be.

So, thank you Father,

For your love,

For me,

No greater lover,

The love of God for we.

9

Look for the Son,

The son that always shines.

He never leaves a shadow,

And never hides behind a planet.

Always there for one,

Give new life in you,

The Son that has woven better,

Never hides,

Always true,

He gives life, abundance, and more.

10

Why do we act superior,

When we are son and daughter?

Of so much more we are,

Than royals.

Yet, we in no way act like them,

Humble we should be,

So steady,

Ready to be,

The light to see.

To bring glory to thee.

To He, that be forever,

The light of all eternity.

Some have eyes to see better,

When God Speaks

Some eyes He has made special,

Eyes that can see the spirit of thee.

The spirit that will always be.

In pure love that you can feel,

If you let go for this love of the ages and kneel,

Into your soul to be,

Let this love of the ages come into you,

And stay with you for all of tomorrow.

Paul D. Sims

11

I alone, I want to be,

I ask you to pray.

Just stay awake and pray.

I go to be alone and pray.

I pray to my father alone,

Just like before He prayed,

But this time blood, sweat, and tears,

For what I must do,

A prophecy told for many years.

A job so big, I was born to do.

Soon, they will come for me,

Oh, what they will do.

Ridicule is the least of them,

When God Speaks

Pain will abound for your soul,

After all the pain and abuse,

I give my life for all that call.

My life to save your soul.

Your soul with the father evermore,

No more to ever wander,

I'd call on the Son.

My life indeed for everyone,

Love will be felt so strong,

Forevermore with the father.

I go after this life and leave,

Death is nevermore.

Love, it flows in and out,

In for me,

And out for all others,

Just call on He who is,

Paul D. Sims

Was,

And will be forevermore.

12

Did we need to go so high,

Yet we still can't touch the sky,

For only love can make you fly,

Love of the one who perfectly made the sky.

Paul D. Sims

13

You gave me the word,

A way into my heart.

Breaking down the door to my soul,

Into the soul of the now saved.

Filling the soul with love,

By the door, now open forevermore.

Goodbye to the door,

That had blocked us from all,

That and so much more,

Only His love can open all doors,

Forevermore.

14

What if His call came this hour?

Would you be ready to be lifted,

By His love and power?

Or be left standing,

Singing a song of pain and sorrow?

For your life will have no light tomorrow.

Just wails of pain,

Oh, so awful.

Only when you try to be lawful,

Try to plan for tomorrow,

Life so short.

But few plan to stay,

Oh, Lord save this soul.

Paul D. Sims

        Let in the bright,

        Prevent the sorrow,

        Let in the light.

        It's love that fills your soul,

        Feel the light,

        So, you can fly tomorrow.

15

Release the spirit,

To the young and to the old.

We want that none should,

Ever not know.

About His glory,

Because they were never told.

All be told,

So, they can be brought into the fold.

Paul D. Sims

16

One table, on left.

Oh no , now I know,

That which was foretold,

In this book of old,

The Bible, in which I was told,

It was in fact the truth,

Oh, but now, how do I save my soul?

For He who comes upon the cloud,

Has already come and gone.

Gone to His father with His bride.

Oh, my soul,

Pray now we must,

And never leave.

When God Speaks

What was told, the Bible in our hearts,

We must hold.

Prepare to look up,

Our gaze upon our God,

In wish our soul,

Wishes to go.

Lord above,

Our God beyond,

The love of all unseen and unknown,

Protect us all father.

I know the pain my mortal body will face,

Because I chose not to believe,

Forgetting to read the Bible,

I will feel no relief,

Till my soul is with you,

Oh Lord, save our souls,

Paul D. Sims

> Help us to see the truth,
>
> For our soul can be saved,
>
> If only we choose,
>
> A life with love and you.

17

If they spent the time with you,

Time I spent in conversation,

Finding out what isn't written in the book.

Things that give feeling,

To what will be felt,

When all time is spent with you,

Eventually, overcome with love from thee.

We will all be caught up to the unseen,

Filled with love and comfort from within.

So much it is to feel,

You are the lamb who sacrificed,

And died for me-

Paul D. Sims

So much we do not understand,

But yet we still believe.

More than the book can show us,

You come in to make it felt,

One day to come to thee,

Forever in our hearts

18

I saw a lamb,

As it entered in,

Coming to heal,

Making hearts complete.

Pain now gone,

Pains now never seen,

The unknown, now known,

And life bought for all days.

Show how you get to the place,

Of salvation,

Healing so complete,

If we just believe.

The lamb whispered love,

Paul D. Sims

So sweet,

Love to forever be,

Never to be forgot.

Always to show lights within,

Always forever flowing,

So smooth,

Giving peace to all,

So wide the river,

How could we not,

Want to be within and around it.

19

I plead inside,

Even though no one sees,

You think that nothing is a matter,

I hide it from my face,

Because my face would give it all away,

Showing what I don't want seen.

You let me show no pain,

You let me show no problems,

They can't tell if it's already fixed,

Or in your care now.

We show the face that shines,

To give a look to you,

For our love of you is larger,

Paul D. Sims

Than the problems that we face,

We built up walls to keep them out,

So that they could not see,

We hide, while you work on what we have,

Building our belief,

Only you can fix, the problems that we speak,

If only we give it all to you.

I plead inside,

Please take it,

Take it all from me,

I cannot carry all the pain,

It drives me to my knees.

It may be to much for me,

But nothing is for you.

You my God, are bigger,

When God Speaks

Only you can carry it all,

You created everything like you.

Thank you for all you do,

Show me what I need of you,

The faces only hide until your works complete,

Leaning on nothing of this world,

But you.

Paul D. Sims

20

So many look for the answers,

Answers they can't find,

They look in places,

Not even in His mind.

The answers that are sought,

They may find that a book of old,

Holds the answers to all their questions.

But the book is years old,

Thousands of years,

Partway old,

Partway new,

Where the answers can be found,

Even those who say it's too old,

When God Speaks

Can find their answers now.

21

Why didn't you ask me to change?

Instead, it's pressure put on me,

Making me feel rejected,

By those I once respected,

For if I wandered away,

It would be easier to see,

What you wanted me to see.

A new place for me,

To help me to do your will.

Preparing me for the job I was born to do,

To do right and in truth,

To show your glory,

And love of you.

When God Speaks

Leading and letting people see,

How bright and shining you really are.

A love of yours,

That calls them in,

I hope they feel your glory too,

For that is what will keep them with you,

You open the doors,

To show us all of what you are,

What you have been,

And will be,

A love all for them,

As it was for me,

To lead us into eternity.

Paul D. Sims

SECTION THREE

When God Speaks

1

Looking into something,

Searching for my reflection.

Not seeing anything,

That looks as I remember.

Pictures of many other people I see,

One stands out among its others.

He looks like someone I've always known,

A friend,

A person,

Paul D. Sims

There when I need,

Someone who saved me,

Someone who cared for me,

Someone whose coming for me.

The one who stands for me,

The one who cares for me,

The one who saved me.

He not only gave me His reflection,

Because of this love I have for Him,

And His love for me,

Greater His love,

Greater His gifts He gave me.

A reflection of He,

When I expected me.

The love He has given,

Reflected back,

When God Speaks

If only we choose to take it.

A Gift abundantly,

Life forever with He.

Paul D. Sims

2

Remember the years,

As they pass you by.

What you have seen,

What you have done,

What have you become?

Is it what you wanted?

Or just something that exists,

A life lived in lies?

Even now there is time,

Time to turn it all around.

Remember the years,

As days pass you by,

Have you seen the hand?

When God Speaks

The hand guides your life.

Or, see the hand,

Pass you by.

It is time to let go,

And quite living the lies,

In your life.

Give your heart to Him,

Whom it belongs.

Give your soul,

To always live on.

Heaven is where,

You belong.

Before it is too late,

Remember the years,

As they pass you.

Never forget to let go,

Paul D. Sims

> So that you may live on,
>
> Live on in eternity,
>
> With He who you belong too,
>
> Live on.

3

The world turns,

Phones ring,

The words of a friend so dear.

Waiting, waiting to hear.

Words of whom we all want to hold near,

Wait till the end is here.

Time comes,

Time goes,

Never to Know.

Within it's here we're going,

Towards all the things we hold dear.

Moments sublime and wanted,

Not a waste of time,

Paul D. Sims

In sight.

Let us run far from fear,

Life goes quickly,

Run faster,

Plans go by, never to appear.

The days are not to fear.

Let us use He who gave His life,

A new and special guide.

Keep Him always near.

Until He comes for us.

Why do some never learn?

How dear,

How sweet,

Our savior to meet,

Come today,

Come to stay.

Come to be life's example.

Come lord,

Come here,

To take us there.

Take us home,

To always be near.

4

Why leave it in your mind,

Why hide it in your heart,

When the message is so kind,

For a world that's torn apart.

So, tell them now,

Tell them right now,

We have so little time.

Life so quickly passes by.

So, tell them here,

Tell them now.

People try so hard to cope,

They need love, joy, and peace.

Won't you share the lasting hope,

When God Speaks

And speak of God's amazing grace?

5

You show my the rainbow,

To show of it's promise.

You gave the light,

Now let us see the glory in which is you.

For us to see the beauty of you,

Love for you we should show,

For only you are worthy.

Never let go,

Hold on tight.

It's your day, feel your power.

Feel your grace,

Feel your glory.

Show us your glory,

When God Speaks

Show us your power.

Show us your love,

This is the hour.

Show us all that we can stand,

Love, love, love is your glory.

Forever you rein through the hours.

Paul D. Sims

6

Been looking into an eye,

A simple cat's eye, defined.

Not a special eye,

Just an ordinary eye that doesn't see.

Not something special that takes away the tears,

Yet when the eye is split inside,

And broken wide.

Bringing life,

Where blindness shines,

Is now a light,

That takes away the fears,

To heal all brokenness,

When God Speaks

If this weren't just a cat's eye.

But instead, an eye of life.

7

We come from worlds apart,

But somehow we found each other.

In a place called the heart,

The soul looks for its other part,

Looking for the missing piece,

In which it can truly be filled,

Never forget oh, how far,

The soul travels for His will.

Looking to complete the heart,

It's time and takes patience,

But there is nothing like a complete heart.

Look at the world,

Big as it is.

When God Speaks

How many hearts to look at,

Just to find the other part.

Keep faith,

For it may not be ready.

Wanting it's other part,

Always searching.

Ask and it will be made ready,

The heart now complete for you.

All complete and perfected by He.

A perfect heart for a human heart,

Unneeded to go searching.

A love everlasting,

Completing the soul,

And made for you and me.

Time will pass,

But you need only ask,

Paul D. Sims

> And you are destined to receive,
>
> That in which your souls longing,
>
> Will achieve,
>
> A love forever more,
>
> A love that we need,
>
> A love for you and me.

When God Speaks

8

Storms a Comin, feel so alone,

Runnin out on my own,

Lost time,

For the last time.

Trying to find my way back home,

Looking hard for the way,

The way back home.

All alone In a place.

That's not my home.

Trying hard to find,

A way to never again be alone.

Look all around just to find,

A book, with a cross on the front.

Paul D. Sims

Two words on the front, the Holy Bible.

The words inside brought to me,

Brought me back home.

Never to be alone again,

Found a friend I had all along.

Now I walk this road no longer on my own.

Instead by His hand, a redeemer,

A leader from heaven above.

Never to be alone,

Or in a separate place,

Forever surrounded by His grace.

9

So many faces,

So many places.

Many close to you,

Many look for you.

In the imagination is you,

We are made by you.

So, again I ask,

So many faces,

From so many places,

Many close to you,

Many look for you.

We look to find you,

We want to see you,

Paul D. Sims

Always and forever with you,

What faces will we see?

When we are with you,

Today I face a problem,

You say I'm here for you,

Yet I see nothing of you,

I ask where are you,

You say you're here for me,

Understand, I cannot,

You say feel my hand,

For it is always on you,

Always I am with you,

Always I love you child,

Always we are together,

My face is no longer farther,

My love, my grace, my way,

When God Speaks

Forever I am beside you,
Forever I have won the day.

Paul D. Sims

10

Why do we love this way?

A way that's incomplete,

Looking past the dream,

Where is Heavens door?

You just wanted one thing from me,

Through heavens door,

You wanted my soul,

To bring my heart new peace,

No longer left alone,

Loving incomplete.

The door, how small it seems,

Can fit my battered soul,

To fill me up with peace and serenity,

When God Speaks

Once certain it was a closed door,

Now we can see,

That time has no beginning or end,

Your will directs it all,

Some doors open,

Some doors close,

And some times there is a wall,

But at all times heavens door is open,

You will never let us fall.

11

So many faces,

In some way,

I can see you,

Little to you as big to us,

So many places,

Feel so big,

Feel so small,

Each showing things of you,

Why with you being so easy to see,

Can't so many see you,

I see you in everything,

Yet other's need your light,

Seen in the smallest things,

When God Speaks

And the biggest things,

The traces of you stand,

Never alone,

Always with us,

Help them see,

You are greatest of everything,

In every day it is all you,

Forever with you,

Show them,

Show them it's you,

Open their eyes and hearts,

Let them see your glory,

Let them know it's you,

Your grace flows in so many,

So many in this place,

In many places With so many faces.

12

I see a light so bright,

The light blinds me,

I can't see with my eyes,

I ask how to see,

Within a light that blinds me,

Given the knowledge to see with my spirit,

My eyes are no good here,

Instead I can see with what never dies,

See with what never lies,

But it's light builds inside.

To shine,

Showing its way,

Yes You light the way,

When God Speaks

The one that's in us,

Let all see the truth,

The truth that is in me,

The truth put in us,

Let it shine bright,

My children,

Let it call all of them,

Let it bring them to Me,

Let the light shine,

Let it shine for me,

Let it bring them to my side,

Let it bring them to the truth,

A light so bright,

It shines the way,

Showing a path back to me,

For you let it shine for them.

Paul D. Sims

13

From the time it began,

Till the time it will end,

From when we enjoy wine,

Till it's time to fly,

Love has a reason to find,

Find every heart,

Find every soul,

The one's in need of more,

Than they had before,

No longer needing to be alone,

A love for all time,

Has shown a love so true,

And never endless,

When God Speaks

It's time to love again,

I have shown the beginning,

I have shown the end,

Never will I leave you alone,

I will love,

I will be there,

Even when you feel so alone,

Desperate and clinging,

Never will you be,

On your own,

I am there in your heart,

And your soul,

Trying to find a way,

To your mind,

Just to tell you,

You're not alone,

Paul D. Sims

My love is always there,

My love will never leave,

Never will you be alone again,

Hearts as one,

Hearts and souls,

Never on their own,

Made in one,

All one to be,

For all time with me my child your Father in heaven.

When God Speaks

14

The eyes speak more than words,

The mouth speaks,

The words the eyes speak,

In God the words for the soul,

Too hear words,

Of both angry and peace,

Words of whispers and division,

Words of man and,

Words of God,

Words of those who love and hate,

The mouth can lie,

The eyes can only speak the truth,

Eyes are tools,

For those who know how to use them,

As God opens the eyes,

They can be shown,

Eyes can show you how to be carried away,

Trust not the mouth,

The eyes are windows to the soul,

Spirit rest in the soul,

Look in the eyes,

See the spirit,

In the soul find the eyes.

Of love,

Of peace,

Of unity.

Find the eyes,

Of a good soul,

A spirit who opens the heart.

When God Speaks

With the eyes follow a good soul,
    No spirit to fly alone.

15

There is something inside us all,

Never mean,

Never wanting to end,

Always loving,

Wanting to be with us,

Till the end,

Days upon days,

One friend, always there,

Till we see everyone,

Days upon days,

Hours by hours,

Years upon years,

Stand with us in eternity forever.

When God Speaks

Always this friend is there.

Love evermore,

Love everlasting,

Grace upon grace extends.

Peace without reason,

Forever given,

From the love of a holy friend.

16

Hold back the tears,

Tears I had for years,

Waiting for someone,

To take the tears,

And give me joy,

For all those years,

Waiting patiently,

Coming into the heart,

Joy fills my soul,

Joy from the son of the Father,

The builder of all creation.

Oh, how He's come to stay,

Now has come to stay,

When God Speaks

In my heart and soul.

Love so strong,

Love that will last,

Never ending yes,

Never again to pass.

17

Floating away on what's never been seen,

Floating to Him,

We should be floating on clouds,

That never will be again,

Carrying us to whom is,

In the end,

In the clouds we go,

Calling our names,

We will be with the King of Kings,

The Lord of Lords,

The Alpha and Omega.

Always to be one in Heaven,

With the Father, Son, and Spirit.

When God Speaks

Carried away on currents,

Currents of winds forever,

Floating in our new body as the Father's treasure.

18

Just you wait and see,

What is to be,

When Jesus comes calling to you and me,

Forever we will be,

Flying high with the Spirit,

With the glory of He who will always be,

Fly to the doorway,

Fly through its doorway,

Filled with the Spirit you must be,

Just to enter through the narrow doorway,

The narrow path you see,

Fly on special winds of the Spirit,

When God Speaks

The doorway to Heaven will be open,

The pathway once narrow in which you seek,

And now wider for you to see,

Fly lifted up by the man you have never seen.

19

Hiding in my mind,

Afraid I am lost in time,

Just trying to hold on.

Give me what's divine,

So if I am lost in time,

I want loss from my mind,

Just a little time,

What should I refine?

To make me feel fine,

Again in body and mind,

Oh, I want life from the divine,

Calling on the Holy Spirit to clear my heart and mind,

Bring my spirit back to life,

When God Speaks

He who is divine.

A love given to me like no other,

Given me life eternal.

Shine this way,

Shine the light,

So bright,

Give me its light,

Call all to you King of my life,

Come to me no longer what's unseen.

20

Looking deep into your eyes,

I see life coming alive,

Just in your eyes,

Light shines brightly now,

Life turns in and turns on,

Coming deep from within,

Put there by a Spirit,

Holy and true,

Now from the eyes,

From every part of its face,

Given a life that flows and flows,

For all to feel.

A driven life never ending,

When God Speaks

Now life for you divine,

Lift up on high,

By a Spirit so Holy,

Survive life now never ending,

Jesus calls all of you to come,

See the light that shines through the Father's eyes.

Paul D. Sims

21

Through this life I carved,

Looking for what never hides,

For what is always around us,

Never hidden,

Whoever asks for it,

He will come into your life,

For all He wants is to give,

Give you life abundantly,

Evermore He gives us a joy unstoppable,

Strange it's normal eyes,

Will today be the day for you?

Will you receive His gift of life,

The gift of sight,

When God Speaks

Not for what's seen,

But what is felt,

Not for what is of this world,

But what is out,

Not for what it is,

But what is yet to be,

What can be,

Let it go,

And reap in which you sow,

Trusting in the Father,

Never ending,

Always living,

Never gone,

Always around,

Always within and always surrounds,

Let it in,

Paul D. Sims

Let it cause you to fly,

Spirit lift you up high.

When God Speaks

SECTION FOUR

Paul D. Sims

1

What if I were to fly,

Straight up into the sky,

Left the earth for the divine,

Let me fly,

Fly high into the sky,

Here I go,

Never to be left alone,

Living this life,

Till the time,

So you and I are ready,

To be lifted high,

Are you ready to fly?

Fly so high,

When God Speaks

Spirit lead us into the sky,

Fly with His glory,

Fly like Elijah and Enoch,

Did they fly to the Lord,

Oh, how they were ready,

Ready to return from the world,

Flying away on the clouds,

With the Lord who led them out.

2

I can feel it in the air tonight,

Can you feel it?

Let it in,

Let it flow,

Right into your soul,

Let it take you over right now,

Ask for it and it's yours,

Are you ready?

Spirit may come,

And is ready to be with you,

Always around,

Always ready,

To new heights you will go,

When God Speaks

Let it in,

Spirit flow,

Love is your guidance,

No longer led by your own defiance.

3

He has always been a good friend,

But you ran too see what was out there,

It's only time that you find,

Drifting quickly by,

When your knees are on the floor,

Pray as you will,

For what you want,

But never gave Him true time of day,

You live life wild,

But this will come to an end,

When you are at your end,

Confronted by your sin,

You will wish you prayed for much more,

When God Speaks

Never living your life like intended,

So now it's time to start,

Before life's expiration date,

The spirit carries on,

Which will pull your heart?

4

So lost,

So alone,

Yet I know this place,

I'm hiding from your face,

Yet I know this place,

A place of my making,

Built with my own hand,

Wow so alone,

So lost.

Will I find what I seek?

It is me in my mind,

This is who it might be,

Life is always running,

When God Speaks

Passing time always going,o
When can I reach the cloud,
Going so fast,
Just flying past,
Am I going to last?
I need a friend to help me through,
A friend that will be true,
But alone and lost I am,
On my knees I fall,
Wanting someone to hear my cal,l
Hear me now calling,
Calling for a friend,
You hear me just before,
I reach my newfound end.

5

I keep feeling lonely,

Missing you inside,

Not knowing,

What is happening,

It's filled me with longing,

Thinking how can I miss what was?

Always to be inside,

Missing a love,

Missing a truth,

I was all love before,

But still it's a love that lasts forever,

Feeling so deep down inside,

Looking for a love of the spiritual kind,

Kept looking for a love that I had the entire time.

6

If I feel something like rage,

Deep in my heart,

Let it be from the Lord above.

Let the rage be from love of God,

Let it be from what He stands for,

To strengthen me,

For let it be love,

Shone from the Lord above,

Let all it lead and be a rage of love,

The power of the Lord's love,

Now as it comes down,

On the world it falls.

Please let us all feel the love,

When God Speaks

Tremble in fear,

But overcome by the peace,

A love that we've never seen,

Causing us all to fall to our knees,

I pray that's what it will be,

If a rage is to come into me,

Let it be from the love of the Lord.

7

Angel you came to my window,

Angel you came to my door,

You came to protect my soul,

I thought you were just another earthly soul,

Just like me,

Tried to send you away.

You kept knocking anyway,

Again and again you came,

Persistent you were,

To save my soul,

Yes you didn't give up,

I didn't know why,

But now I do,

When God Speaks

Protect me you did and still tried knocking,

Just waiting for me to answer,

Angel beautiful you are,

I didn't know who sent you,

But now I do,

Rescued a soul,

Precious in His eyes,

You kept calling for me to come,

No longer suffering,

Or kept from the one who loves for eternity long.

Paul D. Sims

8

Hello again,

Are you sleeping?

Just sleeping on the forever,

Dreaming of eternity,

The type of sleeping you do when dreaming,

Falling and so tired,

Weighed down by my burdens,

Lost in the fire.

No, no, not on my watch.

Not this time.

I can hear a soft calling,

To wake me from my sleep.

Just wake up he,

When God Speaks

He who is sleeping on my watch,
Sleeping without hearing,
Yes so peaceful but not the time,
Time it is to wake,
Wake my resting child,
Now is not the time.
Help!
Please, beating on the chest,
Breathing into his lips,
Trying to wake him again,
No, no, not on my watch,
Death tries creeping in.
Not now you see,
I come to heal,
The calling was clear for him,
Come bring my people here,

Paul D. Sims

Yet this one trying to slide away,

No, no, not on my watch,

Your work here isn't done.

Wake up he,

Who is asleep,

Wishing for those dreams.

Not the time,

Instead, must fly,

Within the Father's light.

Heal my child,

Wake again,

Come into my healing arms,

I wake thee now,

To come forth bound,

Beyond your restful dreams.

When God Speaks

9

What would I do if I were the one,

What would I do if I were Peter?

What would I do if I were Joseph?

Would I stand my ground,

Would I crumble and let him down?

Would I ask what Jesus asked,

Would I ask if this cup would pass?

Never have to do what's hard for me,

We all want to walk through life,

No pain,

No suffering,

No sorrow,

But pain, suffering, and sorrow,

Paul D. Sims

They strengthen and make us strong,

More faith to grow,

Know your love for us wasn't easy for you,

Pain came to you,

So, we could free,

World I stand my ground,

World I stand for Him,

Would I cry for you?

Would I lay my life down for you?

Strengthen me,

Help me walk for you,

Help me stand for you,

Let my love shine through to you,

Always and forever,

For you love flows out from the Father,

Through me,

When God Speaks

To all who need it.

10

Hello again my friend,

Are you there?

I look around outside,

I look everywhere.

Trying to find my lifelong friend,

They say I cannot have a friend I can't see,

A friend they can't see,

I must be wrong in my mind maybe even crazy,

Oh, how wrong they are my friend,

You knew me before I knew myself,

You've been with me from the star,t

From when I asked you to be my friend,

When God Speaks

From then on you've come in,

Where are you my friend?

I feel you are you with me,

Are you more than they understand?

Much more than they can see.

My savior's leading me,

More than they can see.

More than they can understand.

Now I know you are within my soul,

My heart,

My body wake,

Calling for you Lord of Lords,

And so much more you are.

11

How can you see through my eyes,

Into my heart,

Knowing what is in my soul?

Kindling my heart,

Every hole in the past,

Torn apart,

Now fixing it this way,

While looking into my eyes,

Finding a way to bring me back to your side,

For my past kept me from hiding inside,

Wanting what would help me see,

My very soul sends me a new heart,

A new start.

When God Speaks

My life is new,

Because of you,

With this new word,

You gave hope.

Me, no longer keeping us apart,

Together remaking all my parts,

Oh, my soul,

Oh, my heart,

My mind.

Never to be apart,

Without this remade soul,

I would be split apart.

Now I fly with Him,

Making new of my soul and heart.

12

Lord of my days,

God of the way,

God let me be yours

Guide me in all I do,

God keep me close,

Help me be true,

Let me be as close to you as I can be,

Make my heart follow yours,

I long for you and your way,

Keep me,

Guide me and others to you,

You bring them in,

I give them your name,

When God Speaks

I tell of your ways,

You bring them in.

God of my days,

God of the ways,

Let my soul shine,

Let it glow for you,

Bringing glory to your name,

In the darkest night.

Let me fly high with you,

Saving souls,

Forever to be with you too.

Paul D. Sims

13

Is it my time,

To shine bright for you,

do I get to go places I've never been?

On and on I try to stay here and wait,

Calling out to you,

Ready to go.

Has my training come to an end?

Or still in training am I?

Will I see the way through,

To a new day of shining for you?

Going places long ways away,

Ready when you say to go.

Let me hear the beautiful voice,

When God Speaks

Ready am I,

Calling on your ears to hear,

Prepare me,

Prepare me,

Let me get ready to go,

Fly far away,

To do your will,

Bring them to your side,

Let them hear you,

Not me.

Let the voice they hear be yours,

Calling me in to do your will,

My life is your life,

Let it work for you,

My body is your body,

Let it do your will,

Paul D. Sims

Let me shine the light of You.

14

If you were here,

If you were there,

Would it mean you were everywhere?

Or just a person in flight,

Trying to go somewhere light,

Maybe somewhere you've never seen?

Or a place you have not been,

Why do people feel they need to be everywhere,

When it's clear we can only be one place at a time?

So slow down and listen,

For the words from the one who always was,

Paul D. Sims

Always is,

And always will be,

For the one who has the knowledge,

Through the ages,

He wants to show us his way,

The knowledge is free for the asking,

Listen and find what you search for,

He is everywhere and everything,

He will help us fly,

Giving new life in the light,

Replacing the fear in our eyes.

15

Brought me life,

Made me in the womb,

Had a plan for me then,

But I had no clue,

Wish I would have known then what I know now,

What a life I would have had,

Living in you,

For all my life,

Doing your work and your will,

Brought to life by your grace,

Now living with all its worth,

Living in your light,

Basking in your word,

Paul D. Sims

The bright,

Your warmth spreading through me in delight,

Hoping I do right,

In this new life,

You give freely,

Abundantly shining your light,

For then and now,

Helping me to understand,

What it is with you,

Living again,

Your grace,

Your love,

Your way,

Your life given then,

And now let them see its light,

Let it shine forever bright

When God Speaks

16

Wondering where this road is,

The one I am on,

For now is it the one I should be on,

Or just another road I'm on,

What's to be from walking this road?

Is it one I will like,

Or one I will cry about to be on?

Days go on and on,

Walking along,

Trying to see my way home,

How long on this road I will be?

Trying to find a better me,

Or lose what's wrong with me,

When God Speaks

How can it be that a road makes you think so deeply?

Wishing so sweetly,

For things that may never be,

Can I see a fork in the road?

Is it right or left for me?

Let it be.

The best for me,

Let it make the best in me,

More than I can see,

More than I think I will ever be,

Life to be something,

All can see and know,

Whose made it the best,

Make the best in me forever to be with thee.

17

I walked into a dream,

Or so it would seem,

A dream from the past,

But a day I'd never seen,

The past is the past,

Even if it's what I've never seen,

Was it a dream good or bad?

Or something that I'd never had,

Could I walk from the dream?

Or forever be there anyway?

The past come to the past,

The past is where it goes,

Forever to see,

When God Speaks

Never to hold,

Good may happen,

May we wake from the dream,

And leave it be there,

It is to stay for now,

There it is to stay,

From now on never take it home,

Life is but a dream of today,

A vision of tomorrow,

Thought of the past,

All of it gone,

This is what will last.

Paul D. Sims

SECTION FIVE

When God Speaks

1

Just like you,

A kind of newer new,

Longing to no longer be lost,

No longer alone,

Got a friend to help me through,

Make this life worth living,

A friend that's been through it all.

Of it in the past,

Now will it all last ?

Let me see the future I seek,

He says follow me,

I will show you the way,

The truth and the light,

Paul D. Sims

A life like no other,

Last even after this day is done,

Last beyond the sun,

I am here with you forever,

My child come to my side,

I've got you for always and forever,

Today and all the tomorrow's,

See my light.

2

I just opened my eyes from dreams I'd never seen,

Dreams of a place so beautiful,

A place which peace was everywhere,

Oh, the love in this place,

The love of and the feeling from all I see,

Grace flows in this place,

Just open your eyes to see,

And see what a place it will be,

A place of life for all eternity,

To all it will be in this place,

Grace comes from this place,

Spirit, Holy Spirit,

Paul D. Sims

One of this place,

Never to be all again,

Never again to be in pain,

Life bring you here,

A life filled with the Spirit,

Holy Spirit come inside,

Keep me still,

Help us get to this place,

Help us find our way to this place,

Lead us in this place,

Heaven is this place,

Heaven is the dream we seek.

3

Ending love,

For all the years past,

And yet to come,

Love past the tears,

Of love so dear,

Love for all who ask,

Take hold of the given gift of love,

So strong,

Given to all,

To him and him alone,

He gives,

Let all come,

Let him guide you through all the years,

Paul D. Sims

Leave your sorrows behind,

Feel with love,

Instead let it glow inside you,

Let it lift you away,

Make him your world today,

Letting go of what is and what was,

So that you can embrace,

What will be,

For He is what was,

And what is,

And what is to come.

Call him by his name,

The Father,

The Son,

The Holy Spirit,

Call to him by name,

When God Speaks

Jesus called,

Jesus save us now,

Take us in your arms,

Forever far from harm.

Paul D. Sims

4

Tears fall down the face,

Just another lost day,

Oh, what can they do?

Is anyone there that cares?

Anyone to catch the tears,

As each tear falls down,

Heaven calls out,

To the man,

The man who is the only one,

The one who can,

Men and women went through pain,

To one day be saved,

Because of the one who came,

When God Speaks

The one who had his gain,

But souls cry out to the Man,

Call out towards the awesome hand,

With love and glory He shows,

Someone must tell them to cry out,

He catches those tears that fall,

And they give their life to the Man,

Calling out to Him,

Who flies on the cloud above,

He helps to end the pain,

Tell them who He is,

The name,

The name is Jesus,

As He comes,

Pain, sorrow, and suffering will never be again,

God sent His son our way,

Paul D. Sims

> Lest we live for another day,
>
> Eternity in our wake,
>
> Forever loved and saved.

When God Speaks

PSALM 77: 1-20

Paul D. Sims

THE END.

When God Speaks

Paul D. Sims

NEVER FORGET, GOD IS ALWAYS WITH YOU.

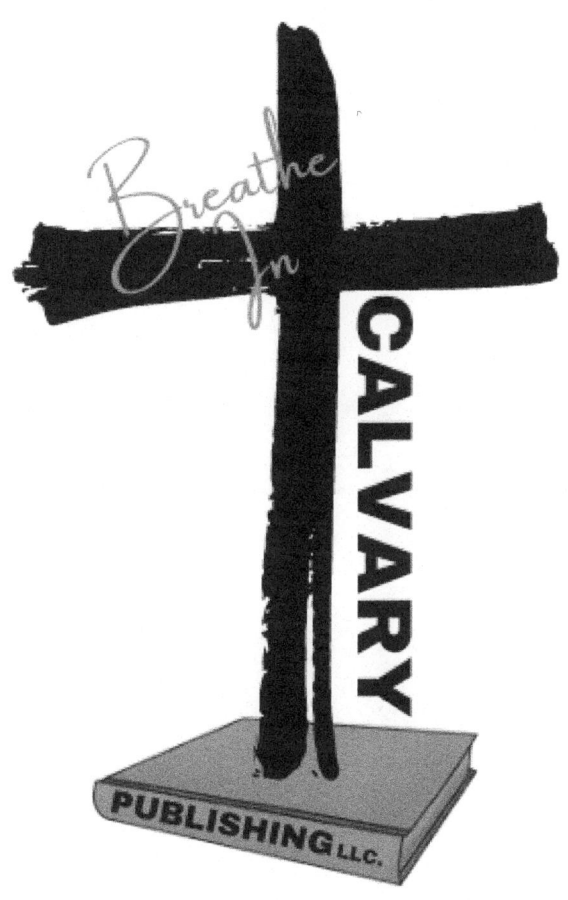

Paul D. Sims

Made in the USA
Monee, IL
10 March 2023